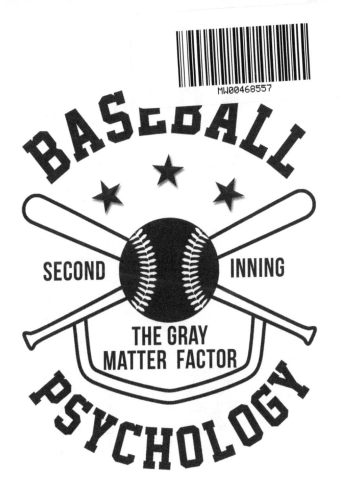

BASEBALL

SECOND INNING

THE GRAY
MATTER FACTOR

PSYCHOLOGY

JACK R. HELBER

STRATTON
—PRESS—
Publishing Life

BASEBALL PSYCHOLOGY:
THE GRAY MATTER FACTOR
Copyright © 2020 **Jack R. Helber**

Stratton Press Publishing
831 N Tatnall Street Suite M #188,
Wilmington, DE 19801
www.stratton-press.com
1-888-323-7009

ISBN (Paperback): 978-1-64895-172-5
ISBN (Ebook): 978-1-64895-173-2

Printed in the United States of America

"Baseball is ninety percent mental and the other half is physical."

—Yogi Berra, Yankee catcher

"What's above the shoulders is more important than what's below."

—Ty Cobb, Detroit Tigers

"He who conquers others is strong. He who conquers himself is mighty!"

—Lao Tzu, Taoist philosopher

"This game is not about how good you are. It's about how you handle failures!"

—unknown

PROLOGUE

Baseball is the most negative game to be played. A 25 percent success rate at the plate has been accepted as an offensive norm, which means that a player can contribute to his team's success by failing 75 percent of the time. It's imperative that players be given methods to combat the negativism that can be generated. Because of the negative aspect of the game, coaches and teammates should always look to find something positive about an *unsuccessful* situation. For instance, a hitter that hits a high *major league* pop-up to the infield with the bases loaded, in reality, just missed by fractions of an inch of hitting the ball on the *sweet spot*. In consoling the player, who obviously is disappointed and distraught, the coach and teammates should point this out to him. It may not make him happy at the time, but it will make him think, *Yeah, I just missed*, and he will be more eager to grab his bat the next time up. The game has enough negativism, so the coach and teammates should not bring more to it. Positive reinforcement will help keep the player in the game and the want to work hard to get better.

If you watched the Olympics and listened to interviews of some of the athletes, especially the gymnasts or divers, you heard them speak of what they had to overcome to get where they are. Most of them spoke of having to defeat *fear* of the event they were involved in before they were able to perform that event; they had to learn to be confident in what they were attempting. The mental side of the sport was just as important as the physical fundamentals. So too, in our sport, baseball, defeating the negative and becoming confident in what you are doing is vital in establishing personal success. Players rely on coaches to teach them the physical fundamentals of the game. What many coaches fail to do is teach the young player the mental fundamentals that he will need to successfully progress through his baseball career. For the young player, the mental part of the game is just as important.

To be athletic takes motor skills and muscle control, but what sets athleticism apart from being merely athletic in a sport is the master of power and control over the *mental* aspect of the game. *Physical* prowess cannot function without *mental* prowess. To most athletes, the mental part of the game becomes the most difficult to master. As has been stated, baseball is the most negative game, therefore the young ball player must learn to fend off all negative thoughts. It is an ongoing process, and he will need help from his coaches, teammates, and parents.

BASEBALL PSYCHOLOGY

Developing the Young Player

Development of the young player must come, at first, from interest created at home. Parents should expose the young child to as many activities as possible, including sports. If this exposure creates a spark in an activity or sport, parents should nurture that spark. Encouragement and patience are key ingredients toward building a long-term interest in the sport. The young developing athlete must receive a satisfaction from his exposure to the activity. In baseball, which entails many negative aspects, it makes it difficult. While working with a young child in baseball, every skill must find a way to become a success. This will take patience on the part of the parent and of the player's first coaches. Work hard to find ways and means to teach the young athlete skills that will help him learn the game. Throw tennis balls up against a wall to practice fielding ground balls. Throw the same tennis balls in the air to practice catching fly balls. For the hitter, there are several drills that can be used to develop that particular skill. The biggest tool any hitter can use, at any level, is a batting T. Hit off the T up against a screen. Move on to what is called a soft toss, with the tosser behind a screen. Use softer practice balls or wiffle balls (Don't throw the T away!). As interest develops, watch the skillful progress of the individual young athlete grow.

Coaches must exercise an extreme amount of patience when working with the young player. The coach must stay positive with every misplay a young player may make. Yelling at the young player will chase him away from the game. It will deflate his confidence and can turn him against the game. Make the misplay a teaching moment. Individual failures should be addressed as a learning experience. Make a failure a positive thing in that it will point out what area needs work. You can mildly criticize knowing the young athlete wants to become a better player, and the criticism is constructive.

Parents put pressure on their young athletes. They should avoid doing that. It is far more important for the young player to learn to love the game, to have fun with it. Allow him to evolve as an athlete, and let the process take care of itself.

> When a boy picks up his first baseball, he picks up much more than just a ball. He picks up a sport, a hope and dreams, a talent, new friends and a

new family, a place to learn life and a place to grow as a person, a place where he can push his limits, gain courage and bravery, and experience lifetime memories. He will gain all of these things simply by picking up his first baseball!

The Personal Batting Average

Most players use the offensive statistic of the batting average as a rule of thumb for success or failure. The *BA* does serve as an indicator to success; however, it can be misleading at times. When a hitter hits a line drive for an out, grounds out hard to an infielder, or is out on a great play by the defense, this lowers his "on-paper" batting average. However, in keeping a *personal batting average,* he should count this as a success, and it will raise his *PBA.* This is not a false statistic. Hitting the ball hard is all the batter can really hope for, and if he is hitting it hard, it will not be counted against him. By keeping a *PBA,* the player can combat feelings of failure at the plate in individual situations. He can also combat real frustrations during streaks where he has hit the ball well several times but has not been credited with a base hit. These times will occur during the season, as every hitter has suffered through them. In arguing that line drive outs are balanced by squib hits, it must be remembered that we are trying to be positive here.

> "You don't have to get a hit to have a good time."
>
> —Joe Maddon

Dotting Averages

Akin to the *PBA* is the *dotting avera*ge. This is an average based on quality at bats with overall plate appearances. (Plate appearances and at-bats are two distinct categories. If a batter goes to the plate, that is an appearance; however if he walks or gets hit by the pitch or sacrifices with a bunt or run-scoring fly ball, that will not be recorded as an at-bat.) When a batter gets any hit, hits the ball hard, drives in a run, successfully sacrifices (bunt or fly ball), advances a runner with no outs, walks or gets hit by a pitch, he will be rewarded with a dot. This dot will be marked next to his name on the dugout lineup card. This will give the player incentive to do well the next time at the plate. ("Coach, did I get a dot for that?") It will also serve to show the player the importance of doing the little things at the plate to help the team's success and will change his attitude about "just getting a hit."

The players will pick up on this statistic and become more concerned and interested in it. It is not a selfish statistic. For the player, it shows interest in how much he is helping his team. For the coach, it will give him a truer picture of how an individual is doing during the game and throughout the season. To find the *dotting average*, divide the total dots by the total plate appearances, including walks, hit batters, and sacrifices. Keep this statistic throughout the season so that you can maintain a truer idea of each players productivity at the plate. An average of .450 or above can be considered a very positive dotting average.

> "Baseball is like Zen. Zen is the philosophy of reducing the elements into total harmony, and what is more in total harmony than eyes, hands, and body coming together to meet a speeding ball? Doing something perfect, that is Zen in a nutshell."
> —Tetsuharo Kawakami,
> early Japanese baseball star

Close Your Eyes and Visualize

Visualizing can be a key to combating the negative aspect of the game. After a player has had a successful at bat, or made a great play, or pitch, he should close his eyes and see that hit, play, pitch a second time, recording it in his *memory bank*. Watch a player point to the sky or beat his chest while he is recording what he has just done so that he can withdraw it during times when things may be going tough. "You have been successful, so see that success again before you go to the plate or take the field." This is positive reinforcement from within and should be used in the future. It can transfer into a real successful physical experience and should take some of the pressure off of a trying situation. This is post-performance visualizing. However, using the visualizing technique before a performance such as hitting or pitching can also be a useful tool. While on deck, draw out from your *memory bank* past successful performances that you have had and see or review them again. Do this a second time before you step into the batter's box. This will remind you of prior successes and will help you to compete at a higher level with more self-confidence. Pitchers can do the same when they need to make a key pitch in at a critical moment. If you are a fielder, you can also use this technique prior to a pitch, especially in critical moments.

Visualizing can happen two ways. In some instances, visualizing a mistake or poor execution can help to make sure that the mistake will not happen again. As an example, a pitcher may get an out on a pitch in the hitter's wheelhouse. He will not want to make that pitch again, and visualizing this mistake will help him to not repeat it.

Another version of visualizing, and one that many excellent athletes use, is *daydreaming.* Off the field and in spare moments, they will see themselves in tough situations and mentally view how they can get out of that situation, or defeat the problem by *dreaming* of their action. This then can translate into an actual on-field moment, and they will be able to use this *mental practice* for a successful defeat of the situation. Visualizing works as subliminal reinforcement before and after actual act.

"Seeing is believing!"

Picking Up Your Teammates

Players and coaches should *pick up* their teammates after they have had a *negative success.* (Hitting a rocket for an out is a negative success.) The player's teammates should greet him with a hand shake or pat on the back when he returns to the dugout, giving positive feedback. Coaches should see to it that this happens. This positive encouragement can occur even after a strike out or other not-so-glorious at bat. Players should continually encourage each other as it can only help keep up the spirit of the team. This is a basic foundation of a successful team. Team spirit creates togetherness whereby each player begins to fight for his teammate before considering himself. The team becomes "one" as opposed to a group of individuals. Each player will go through difficult times during the game, season, and career. To get past these times, the player will need help from his teammates and coaches.

> "You look at championship teams and you see that the players take a lot of responsibility for the way they play."
>
> —Luke Walton, LA Lakers

Funk versus Slump

Avoid using the word *slump* as it has earned a too negative meaning of continued failure. Rather, use the word *funk* because as every player has had negative periods, they have also gone through very positive times. A player in a slump seems to dwell on the negative, "I can't." Whereas, a player in a funk has done it before (visualized), so he knows he can do it again. "Geez, I'm in a funk." The use of funk to replace slump will put, into the player's mind, an attitude to work harder to defeat the *funk*. In a slump, the player will have the tendency to give up or develop an attitude of defeat. It becomes a downhill slope for the individual and will cause the player to lose playing time. The coach's attitude will be to sit the player for a couple of games so to give him some time to think about his situation, not allowing him to fight his way out of the *funk*. Substituting the word *funk* for the word *slump* may be a play on words, but the mind can be affected by the interpretations of these words, and the mind is what we are dealing with here.

> "There are no bad days. Just different types of good days!"
> —Col. Sanders, Chicken King

Watch the Other Guys

The biggest tool in learning how to play is to watch the major leaguers—*the cream of the crop*. When a player watches a game, he will invariably study the hitters and players at his position. Many times, he will imitate what he sees. This is good, for it is how he learns. But how many times has a player or coach groaned about the execution of a certain play, at bat, or pitch that he or his team has made in a game? And how many times has the player or coach gone home and watched a major league game on TV and seen a player do virtually the same thing? It happens quite often. Major league players are not perfect; they are just better, or sometimes the best, at what they do. But no one has ever turned in a 1.000 batting average or 1.000 fielding average, or a perfect pitching record. Hard work has gotten the big leaguer where he is. Positive feelings about their ability has helped them to a higher level of performance.

On the youth level, the same thing is true. The player should approach the game with the attitude that, *I know I will not be perfect 100 percent all the time, but my job is to work hard and improve my percentages.* If you work hard every moment for excellence, it can become a habit. Every single game, practice, or workout offers an opportunity to learn something, just by watching. Sometimes you have to see the big picture of the game. When you are on the field, you have a tendency to get locked-in with tunnel vision. Make the most of the games in which you *don't* play. Coaches should require young players to watch a game on television or in person every week. Those games can include the little brother's games, any game! Watch and learn! Some small aspect of the game can be learned just by watching someone else play. All players should learn something from every game they see.

Wisdom and knowledge are gained by what has been learned and observed. Listen to words that are spoken when a coach is working with an individual. Select what works and what you like and make it a part of you. Make the game a study. "Baseball smarts" are more than turning information gained into knowledge. Rather, it is the ability to sort through the knowledge, mixing it with judgments and experience, and then applying what has been learned on the field, at the plate, or on the mound. These are the main ingredients in gaining *baseball sense*.

A perfect example of studying the game is that of Kirk Gibson of the Los Angeles Dodgers versus the Oakland A's in the 1988 World Series. Scouts had covered the A's during the regular season and had determined that the ace reliever, Dennis Eckersley, would throw a certain pitch (backdoor slider) on special counts.

The Scouts passed this information to the Dodger players. Gibson was injured and not expected to play early in the series. Nevertheless, in the first game of the series, he was called upon to pinch hit in the bottom of the ninth inning with the Dodgers trailing 5–4. There were two out and one runner on base. Gibson made a few feeble attempts at a couple of pitches, hobbling out of the batter's box on one occasion, but fouling off some good Ekersly pitches. He worked the count to 3–2, a count in which he recalled the scouts said Ekersley would throw his slider. Gibson was looking for the pitch and got it and slugged a two-run home run (almost one handed by the way). This gave the Dodgers the first game victory of the series in which they went on to win. This is truly another example of being prepared—scouting, taking notes, reviewing them, and acting upon them.

> "It's what you learn after you know it all that counts!"
>
> —John Wooden

The Gray Matter Factor

A hard ground ball is hit to the shortstop for an apparent easy double play, but he boots it. How he immediately reacts to this misplay is a key to what can happen later. "Someone with good *self-confidence* knows that it is part of the game and at some level accepts it." "Great athletes have short memories." They can forget their mistakes, and even the emotion of their successes, to *focus* on the immediate moment. This is not to say that they are not concerned with making the error, but it allows them to immediately continue without emotional hindrance. This is *mental control*, and it comes with maturity. But maturity is not measured in age; it is developed. A player must learn to realize the importance of control of tension and stress. A player cannot not fully operate under stress or in tension-filled moments. Batters must hit tension free. Pitchers must pitch tension free. Development of self-confidence is a vital ingredient toward reducing tension-filled moments. A disciplined ball player can only help develop a more disciplined team. There are several methods found in this text that you can use to help alleviate tension.

"It's not a crime to get knocked down
in life…it's a crime to not get up!"

BASEBALL PSYCHOLOGY: THE GRAY MATTER FACTOR

Beware of the Little Man Inside

This plays right along with the *gray matter factor.* Within the subconscious in all of us, there is a *little man* telling us what is or what is not. This man operates on the intangibles known as *fear, frustration,* or *self-pity.* He can tell you that you are not "good enough" to master a situation. He can tell you that the other guy is better than you. He will instill all kinds of negative thoughts. He is like a virus that builds inside to the point that you are afraid to face a situation, make a move, or decision. If you listen, he will become a powerful force in your psyche. You can combat this virus through various steps suggested in this text such as "Self-talk," the "Positive Rectangle," or "Visualization," especially if you have done something with a positive outcome in the past.

The power of positive thinking becomes a major prescription for the cure of this virus. Instead of a negative reaction to a failure, make a commitment to be positive. Use past positive experiences to help you do this. Build on the little things. Manage those things over which you have control, such as your performance, and embrace the challenge of the game with respect to it. *Live the moment. Control what you can control. Don't get ahead of yourself. Expect the unexpected.* Building *self-confidence* through the use of some of these tools can turn the *little man* into a positive force in how you perform. For maximum performance, you must have the *little man* on your side.

"You can't be afraid to make errors. You can't be afraid to stand naked before the crowd, because no one can ever master the game of baseball. You can only challenge it."

—Lou Brock, St. Louis Cards

When you go between the lines, that's what you must do!

Self-Talk

Inner conversations with oneself can be a valuable tool to motivate an athlete in tense moments. He can create a state of well-being by recalling positive thoughts of past successes during these testing times. As a result, self-talk becomes a key factor in the athlete's approach to the situation at hand. It will also become a major component in defeating the challenge posed by "the little man inside." Many players inscribe messages under the bill of their cap or in the lining. Why do they do this? Obviously, it is another method of communicating with oneself—another method of self-talk.

In a tough situation, he can easily take off his cap and reread the written message. After all, no message would be written if the player did not believe in it or if the event referred to did not happen. This goes back to the text on visualizing. A combination of "reseeing" a positive consequence, and of referring to positive thoughts before an actual event occurs, can give the athlete a more confident, controlled approach to what may be due to happen. Hitters should talk to themselves on deck or in the batter's box; pitchers should talk to themselves on the mound; fielders do the same at their position. Lips don't have to move for it is an inner conversation that prepares you for the near future. Develop a personal mantra—a short positive saying that you can repeat to yourself in difficult moments. Something simple that can be remembered easily, but with a good positive meaning. You can make this a lifetime mantra.

> "I will be the same person if I get a hit or make an out. I'm good when the chips are down!"
> —Al Oliver, Pirates

The Tennis Ball Effect

When a player has had a bad inning or is having a bad game (couple of errors, o-fer, etc.), and there will be those days, he can come into the dugout, take out a tennis ball that he has kept in his bag, go down to the end of the bench, and bounce it once, reassuring him that he is better than what he has done today and that he can bounce back! This is such a small gesture to oneself but can be key to the mental resurrection of confidence in his ability. In reality, this is another method of self-talk. Each player can create his own method of reassurance, but it is absolutely important for him to get back to a mental state of confidence. This gesture of using a tennis ball can also save the player from hurting himself or destroying equipment during an outbreak of self-dissatisfaction. A coach could place a team tennis ball somewhere handy in the dugout for any player who returns to the dugout after a bad outing at the plate, mound, or in the field. He should then insist that the player use it to calm his frustration in a more disciplined mental exhibition of that frustration.

"Forget the past. Create a future!"

The Positive Rectangle

Confidence is a key to success for a young player. But confidence is continually fighting off the challenges of that great intimidator, *fear.* Fear can show up at almost any time, especially when a struggling hitter faces a pitcher that he rates as superior. Here is where the hitter uses the batter's box (*the positive rectangle*) as his sanctum from fear. When he steps into the batter's box, he must shed any feelings of fear from an overpowering pitcher. He must realize that he is in the box because he has earned it, that he has been successful in the past and he will be successful again. If he has any inclinations of fear, he must step out of the box, gather himself, and step back in only after he sheds the negative emotion. Inside the box there can be no fear. It is replaced by *respect*, of course, making the confrontation a challenge. Respect for a pressure situation, rather than the fear of it, serves to overcome the negative *emotion* and *anxiety* that can develop, and it will assist the athlete in gaining success and control over the situation. The pitcher can use the same tactic while on the mound. He will not step onto the rubber—his *positive rectangle*—until he has cleared his thoughts of any negativity. Players in the field can use an imaginary rectangle, stepping out of it after a pitch and back into it when the pitcher is in his wind-up. Keeping emotions under control will go a long way toward keeping the body under control. The *positive rectangle* is an important aide in achieving this control.

> "Success is developed through confidence and belief."

The Beauty of "Do"

When a player goes to the plate with a thought of *don't* do something such as, "Don't take a certain pitch for a called third strike," he will invariably freeze on that pitch and be called out on it. He must substitute the negative *don't* with the *beauty of do*! This positive will increase his chances of creating action on the pitch (swinging), and success will be greatly enhanced. The player should *self-talk* with positive thoughts, especially with that in which he has trouble. "I want that inside pitch because I'm going to get my hands through quickly and yank it!" *Want to!* This is *the beauty of do!* However, these positive thoughts by the hitter does not mean he should just swing at all strikes. He should wait for his particular pitch and jump on it when he sees it. Shrink the zone to what you are looking for. When he does this, the *beauty of do* will click in because he is ready. *Do* applies to each aspect of the game. Pitchers pitch with positive "I can" or "I will" make this pitch, rather than, "Don't walk him." Fielders do the same, "I can make this play." This positive feeling starts in practice when the player works hard in drills—fielding, hitting, pitching, running. This is where the player develops his proficiency and positiveness, which he will take with him when going onto the field in a regular game.

The *beauty of do* and its positive approach extends to the dugout. Hitters and pitchers should receive positive responses from their teammates in the dugout when they are at bat or on the mound. A batter with two strikes on him should hear positive comments extolling confidence rather than a negative, "Don't strike out." The same goes when a team's pitcher is on the mound who has a three ball count on the opponents batter. Teammates should encourage their pitcher to, "come back and get him;" as opposed to pleading for their pitcher to not walk him. This approach is imperative for both the individual player and his teammates. It helps create a feeling of team support and togetherness in a positive atmosphere.

> "Go confidently in the direction of your dreams."
> —Henry David Thoreau

Developing Swag

Swag is a key element in a player's ability to handle tough moments and times. It is a feeling of confidence in any situation that should arise, and in baseball, they can arise instantaneously. But *swag* must be developed by creating a winning emotional aura about oneself, or confidence in one's ability. It is an inner swag, as opposed to an outer swag, which can be interpreted negatively as boasting or false bravado. Inner swag, or lack of it, can easily be seen by observing body language—how a player reacts to a tough situation. To develop this inner swag, the player must play the game "one pitch at a time." A critical variable is to realize that baseball and its individual circumstances are *fun* as opposed to being *threats*. The player must free himself from a belief system based on *fear* and turn to a belief system based on *love* and *respect for the game*. Once a player can develop these concepts, he will then be able to put to use the ABCs of emotional control—*swag*! He will *act* big—not be nervous, but be up for the challenge; *breath* big—show inner control of mind and body; and *commit* big—want the action to come to him. The cry should be, as a fielder, "Hit it to me," or the hitter, "Throw me your best pitch," and the pitcher, "Here it comes, hit it if you can!"

The negativity in baseball is huge, and the player must constantly battle fearful emotions. The ones that can do this will continue in the game with greater chances to advance to a higher level. If a player can develop this *swag*, it will be very difficult to best him in any endeavor in life. The importance of an inner swag cannot be underemphasized. The projection of confidence can affect the opponent's demeanor and approach to a tough situation that he may be facing, causing him to make a wrong decision.

> "This confidence is a fascinating commodity. There is no upper limit to the usefulness of it, as long as it doesn't bleed into arrogance."
> —Jerry Seinfeld

Baseball's Three Demands

The game of baseball makes many demands on the individual player and his teammates. The younger player will not realize these demands early in his career, but as he progresses throughout his career, he will learn that this game can be very demanding. In the beginning, the young player will find that it demands time to practice and play. His parents will become involved with time also, including transportation and support. As the player's experience grows, these demands will change, and the true demands on the field will develop. These on-field demands will include *courage*, *intelligence*, and *hustle*, among others.

Courage to battle one's way through difficult times on the field. The courage to act on your own ideas and make your own decisions on the field. But more importantly, individual courage to fight off all kinds of negativity, which will become part of the game for him. Courage to fight through tough times at the plate when he has not been successful for a period of time and begins to think that maybe he can't play this game. Courage to want the ball hit to him again after booting the ball in the field during a crucial moment. Or for the pitcher, the courage to get back on the mound after a misplaced pitch causing a successful moment for the opposition. Even, as a base runner, getting picked off ending a critical rally for his team. Each one of these situations, and many other negative moments, can and will cause the player to become distraught, believing he has let his team down. The young player must learn to overcome these feelings and have the courage to rebound. He must learn to take chances on the field, have the courage to attempt a difficult play (see "You Gotta Jump"). The courage to "go for it" is essential in the development of the successful athlete. Any successful attempt of a difficult play can only increase the players confidence, which must be developed by him in order to advance to the next level. *What you fear is what you will create.* The confidence and belief in one's ability is absolutely necessary for this advancement. You gain strength and confidence through every experience in which you look fear in the eye. You lived through it so you can master the next fear that arises. You will do that which you believe you cannot do! That takes *courage!*

Another demand from baseball is *intelligence.* A player must learn that *he* is playing the game, and it is he who must make the important decisions on the field. Coaches can flash offensive and defensive signs to help the player, but the individual player must concentrate on the game so that he will learn, himself, what he can do in certain situations that may arise. Each decision could become the most important one toward the success of the team in the game. After all, making important decisions on the field is the most critical action a player must do. Through playing and gaining experience, the player will retain information he has gathered, to acquire baseball "smarts," and be ready to react to any situation that may arise on the field. This is the *intelligence* that the player will need to continue to a higher level of play (refer to the section on "Constraints and Complexities"). Constraints, and complexities that they cause, will appear several times in an individual's career. The knowledge that a player gains in how to survive unwanted situations will give him a tremendous advantage in overcoming constraints when they occur. Intelligence and knowledge, gained through experiencing tough situations, will become of major importance in the development and advancement of the individual's career.

Finally, the third essential demand of baseball is *hustle. Hustle is a talent!* It will inspire your teammates and will contribute to the "pulse" of the game. Hustle creates team spirit and, *spirit will take you beyond your wildest thoughts and dreams!* By hustling, you are telling your teammates you want to win. Hustling can become a communicable disease by sparking your teammates and causing them to do the same. It will lead to a better ball player and better teammates by increasing the desire to learn in practice and play harder in games. It creates a competitive atmosphere in practice. *Physical hustle* includes running out every fly ball, performing wind sprints to the maximum, working hard in drills no matter how boring they may become, and working hard in the cages even when no coach is nearby. *Luck is the residue of hard work*. Get lucky!

Mental hustle includes interest, enthusiasm, aggressiveness, and single-mindedness toward reaching a goal. Watching the game from the dugout, whether you are in the lineup or not, will help you to learn something early in the game that you or your team can use to win later in the game. Part of the game is the ability to study what is going on and pass it on to your teammates. This is a major component of *mental hustle*.

These three demands are essential in the development of the young ballplayer. He must take them to heart and work diligently and tirelessly on them in order to progress to the next step, and the steps beyond.

"A true warrior lives in the process.
There is no fear in the process."

The Want and the Will

It starts young. Young players will say that they *want* to play baseball. They start in Little League and go on to travel ball, or some other higher league where the competition becomes more intense and the game becomes more difficult and faster. Some will drop out at some point. Those who continue on will discover that baseball is more complicated and will require more work, more practice, and more knowledge. This is where the *will* to play begins. Competition among teammates becomes more intense. For the player to continue to advance in the game, he must develop the *will* to do that which will keep him on the field—a work ethic. It will take desire, hard work, and practice. Monotonous repetitions of ground balls, fly balls, hitting in the cages with various drills, getting into shape, and staying in shape is required. If the player wishes to advance to the highest level that he can attain, he must have the *will* to work hard on his craft—fielding his position(s), hitting, and pitching. The want to play is a start, but it is the will to play that keeps the young player in the game.

"The mind is a powerful tool. Will,
and you can climb any mountain."

Row Your Boat

This should be an easy but important concept to understand. Simply put, whatever happens on the field, or in life, you must keep *rowing your boat* downstream. If the event is a negative one, it is important to *not* let it stop you from going forward. Stay focused and determined to continue, knowing that every experience is part of the game, or life. If the event is a positive one, celebrate quietly, realizing that the goal that has been set has not been reached, and that can only occur if you continue to *row your boat.* If you are able to learn to keep an even keel, or keep emotions under control during both negative and positive events, this will aide in the development of a *swag*, or feeling of confidence.

Emotions are acceptable in both negative and positive experiences, but they should not be allowed to get out of control, or "rock your boat," as you continue downstream. In reality, when you row your boat, you actually have your back to where you are going. The same in playing a game or season, you don't know what is ahead. This fits perfectly with the *row your boat* philosophy because as you go "downstream," you really don't know what could be coming around the bend—still water and smooth sailing, or white water where you must watch out for rocks or eddies.

In baseball, it's the next play, the next pitch to hit that you are going to have to deal with. You must be prepared for anything that could happen. This takes mental control (*maturity*—see "Gray Matter Factor"), which is gained when you learn how to maintain your emotions in all situations. When you can accomplish this, you will be able to *row, row, row your boat gently down the stream (of life), merrily* (positively) because life is but a *dream.*

"To rise above adversity does not build character. It reveals it!"

You Gotta Jump

"You gotta jump! You cannot stand on the precipice and do nothing. *You gotta jump* if you want to soar! You gotta take that leap of faith. Jump! be confident that your parachute will open and you will land on your feet! At first, when you jump, your parachute may open late and you will land with scrapes and bruises. But trust your parachute that when you do pull the chord, it will open and you will land safely. Every successful person has jumped. Every successful person has identified their *gift of life* because they have jumped!"—Steve Harvey

Baseball Interpretation

Don't be afraid to attempt to make a difficult play on the field. Have faith in yourself, knowing that your teammates (your parachute) will have your back. It's possible when you attempt something, it may not be successful at first, but you gotta go for it. Every successful player has *jumped*. This is how he identifies his gifts and abilities. This is where he knows what he has to do, what he has to work on, to improve his gifts. All along, his teammates will be with him to help him land on his feet. *None of this will happen if you don't jump!*

BASEBALL PSYCHOLOGY: THE GRAY MATTER FACTOR

"If you won't or don't, how do you
know if you can?"

The Glass of Water

Hold a half glass of water out at full arm's
length. Is it half full or half empty? It's both, but that
is not the lesson here. Hold it out for a while and it
will start to feel heavy. Hold it out a little longer and
your wrist and fingers will start to tense up. If you
continue to hold it out, your wrist and fingers and
arm may begin to ache, and you may, at some point,
start to "lose a grip" and drop it, where it will crash
and break. This is the *physical*.

The same thing can occur when you hold onto
a negative thought or a grudge, or believe that you
"can't." If you hold onto that negativism long enough,
you will begin to tense up. Your heart will begin to
ache, and at some point, you will start to believe that
negativism and "lose a grip" on yourself and "crash
and break." This is the *mental*.

*Put the glass down! Put that negative out of your
mind!* To help defeat that negative thought, call upon
the many positive experiences you have had, especially when they apply to the games you have played
in the past, where you have had successes. You have
been successful, you can do it again!

"Every negative thought you have
releases a poison into your system."
—Willie Nelson

Walk the Walk, Talk the Talk, Dream the Dream

All athletes strive to become the best at their game, position, or individual sport. This is a great ambition, but few actually achieve that goal. Physical ability can be one of the reasons, but more than likely, it's the mental aspect that stands in the way. High levels of achievement will not come easily. The greatest barrier to success is psychological. It will take hard physical work and, most of all, hard mental work. Aspiration can be attained only if you believe you can reach your goal. This belief solely comes from the mind. In baseball, the player must visualize himself, in the performance of a skill, over and over again. He must *talk* himself through the activity—hitting, fielding, pitching—as often as possible. He must *dream* of success as often as he can—daydream if you will—and he must *walk* himself through the performance over and over. This pursuit of success is very demanding, but when it is accomplished, it is hugely rewarding. The player must love the intensity it takes, he must cherish its moments, and he must be ready to accept the risks that may be involved. Competing on the field will help the player to enhance his abilities because it will give him the opportunity to perform what he has envisioned and to extend that performance by "jumping" (see "You Gotta Jump"). Thus, making bigger and better plays with less and less fear. By walking, talking, and dreaming, and then competing and finding success, the player will soon begin to clear his mind of any anxieties, free of any negative thoughts. It is then that he will be able to perform to his utmost ability.

> "Dream big! And focus on your dreams!"
>
> —Clark Apuada,
> ten-year-old swimmer

The "Yips" and Focus Battle It Out

First, we must define the two concepts; they are in opposite dugouts in baseball. The *yips* are a blockage in the brain, a brain freeze if you will, that causes a player, who is otherwise a good athlete, to be unable to perform a certain function. For instance, two classic cases of the *yips* in major league baseball were Steve Sax (1981–1994), a second baseman for the Dodgers, Yankees, and White Sox, and Chuck Knoblauch (1991–2003), another second baseman for the Twins, Yankees, and Royals (by then he had been converted to an outfielder). Knoblauch won a Gold Glove Award for the Twins in 1997. Both developed the *yips* when throwing to first base on a ground ball to them at 2B. Both had great difficulty throwing with accuracy. More than once, the ball landed in the stands behind first base. Obviously, being able to make a major league roster showed that these players were highly athletic, physically. Their problem was not physical but, rather, a psychological breakdown—*the yips.*

This breakdown is developed when a player begins to doubt his ability or puts worrisome thoughts in his head when he is about to perform a function—throwing, hitting, or pitching. In the above cases, these thoughts could have grown after a first bad throw and just continued to increase. Thoughts of, *Don't screw it up again*, or *Don't throw it away*, may have set off the psychological *yips* (see "The Beauty of Do").

Some methods in combating the yips can be found in this text. *Visualizing*, using *the positive rectangle* or circle, replacing *fear* with *respect*, and *love for the game* can help. *Self-talk* or reciting your *positive mantra* may help to rid the yips. The concepts in the next paragraph on *focus* can become invaluable in helping to defeat the *yips*.

Opposite the yips, in the other dugout, so to speak, is the ability to *face our challenges under* stress (FOCUS). Concentration is what is necessary on the field or at bat. To young players, this may become difficult because they have not spent time in seemingly tough situations and can easily be distracted by outside forces—mom, dad, girlfriend, etc. *Focus* takes immense practice and *maturity*, and only those who can master this task will continue to grow in the game. A competitive athlete will take a difficult situation and make it a challenge, *focus* on it to determine what it will take to overcome the situation. Positive thoughts, and the knowledge that success in these situations have occurred, are what must be dwelt upon to begin to eliminate these yips.

> "Build self-awareness. Listen to yourself, change your thoughts, redirect your focus to things inside yourself."

The Theory of Constraints and Complexities

The Theory of Constraints is a book by Dr. Eli Goldratt concerning business and was referred to, recently, by Mark Riffey in an issue of the Flathead Beacon. This text gives its message a baseball slant. Constraints are those things that you weren't expecting. Complexities are the situations that they cause. They are a part of the game that doesn't turn out as you had planned, or when you expected. The smallest things can turn momentum against you at the least opportune time—an error, bad call by the umpire, mislocated pitch. These constraints create unwanted complex situations that threaten the successful completion of that moment or game.

As a player, you must be ready to fight through these complex moments because they happen all the time. Create a checklist of support personnel and methods to help reduce or eliminate a problem that may threaten the safe execution of the immediate situation. The player should resort to his checklist and his support personnel—teammates and coaches. Therefore, it is imperative that the player develop a particular plan or system to help him through any complex moment. He must plan ahead and be ready to employ his system when the "expected" unexpected arises. Where every little "bump in the road," miscalculation, unexpected result, timing problem, or change introduces a chance to fail. This is the basic philosophy of the *theory of constraints and complexities*. If the preparation you take and the plans you make produce continual success, you can expect to overcome the complex constraints that you may be faced with. You must be prepared.

The beauty of complexities is that they can have negative impacts on your opponent as well. Here, you must be able to seize the moment and take full advantage of it. As mentioned, some of these complexities are small, and you must be *focused* on the game in order to recognize them and take the advantage that they can provide. Good teams will be ready for these moments. Overcoming *constraints and complexities* should be a challenge. If you are prepared individually, and your team is prepared, both should experience greater success.

> "The real glory is being knocked to your knees and then coming back. That's the real glory. That's the essence of it."
>
> —Vince Lombardi

The Frank Sinatra Syndrome

"That's life. That's what all the people say, you're ridin' high in April, shot down in May. But I know I'm gonna change that tune, when I'm back on top in

June!" (a song sung by Frank Sinatra). How do you handle challenging situations on the field or possibly a failure to perform? Your response is what will keep you on the field or put you on the bench. Here are six questions to ask yourself:

1. Can I deal with *slumps* (an outlawed term in this text)?
2. Can I get up and bounce back quickly?
3. Am I resilient and can I sustain that resiliency?
4. Can I overcome a setback and make it a learning experience?
5. Can I substitute a self-doubt with a positive self-belief.?
6. Can I sustain a positive attitude during tough turbulent times?

If you have experienced any of these situations (haven't we all) and you were able to answer *yes* by your physical and mental responses, it will make you a stronger tougher player. If you answer *no* to any of these questions, you must work to educate your mind so that you can be able to change your answers to *yes*. Many of the ideas in the text above may be able to help you defeat the negative responses to one or more of these questions. The sound ballplayer must have *confidence* and *assurance* on and off the field. Be true to yourself with the answers. The old adage, "What doesn't kill us makes us stronger," can be used as a self-determination as to how you respond to the above questions. When its baseball season, *get back on top in June*!

> "Perserverence is failing nineteen
> times and succeeding the twentieth."

The Curse of Talent

Certain types of talented young players have trouble with failure, and they deem failure as a public humiliation. What they must learn is perspective—that baseball matters, but it doesn't matter too much! Of course, many young players have dreams of playing in the big leagues. This exacerbates the problem because they feel that someone is always following their progress, and that may be true. They feel that a failure (strike out, error, etc.) can destroy their dreams. "What matters most is that I play flawless." The vicious downhill spiral begins. In actuality, what matters most is that he behaves impeccably when he competes. No game should become "too big." No at bat should become the biggest or most important. Stay under control and react like it's any other game or at bat. Don't allow the thinking process to overshadow the reacting process. Stick with a normal routine. It remains up to his coach to instill the championship types of intangibles in the young player. This list includes the ability to adjust, adapt, and adopt.

Self-control in highly competitive moments, created by development of a better *self-image*, is an important key. Teach the player to "don't try too hard," let nature take its course. Tell him to be natural, don't force it. Be competitive, with control. Teach them that *failure* is part of the process. You won't know where you are vulnerable until you fail. The greatest fear should *not* be failure. The greatest fear should be in succeeding in things that don't matter. Use the many ideas expressed in these writings to help the young player develop and advance to a higher level.

> "Show me a player who has never failed, and I'll show you a mediocre player."

Wa

You Gotta Have Wa is a book by Robert Whiting describing the Japanese baseball cultural philosophy of *group harmony*. It is the very opposite of individualism. This *wa* is described in the proverb, "The nail that sticks up shall be hammered down." Developing the philosophy of group harmony, or team togetherness, will aid in creating an atmosphere of pulling for each other and rooting for teammate's successes. Each success of others can only lead to a better outcome for the team. The spirit of *wa* can also help develop an individual player's positive attitude during difficult moments of the game. A major part of this culture is that every man works diligently toward his improvement for the benefit of the whole. Baseball is a team game in its own unique way. There can be an individual action, but it is usually followed by a teamwork action—double play, basic ground out, pitcher to catcher, fly ball with runners on base. (A fly ball to the outfield with runner at second can put at least six players into action.) To perform these actions throughout a game, no player can be more important than any other player; the team must act as a whole. This is *wa*! It is imperative that coaches develop this spirit of oneness. It is imperative that each player work hard individually and root for his teammate to do the same.

"If you want to go fast, go by yourself.
If you want to go far, go together."

Take a Deep Breath

Tension, anxiety, fear, and any negative emotion can dictate an athlete's approach to the situation. The young player must overcome this negativism and develop a positive approach. Several methods have been mentioned in this text. But a physical activity that the player can use to ease the effects of these mental obstructions is to learn the importance of breathing. It is such a valuable physical action, that it is mentioned with its own paragraph here. It is an action that can go a long way toward erasing the mental interference by these intangibles. Hitters must hit tension free! To aide in this, they can take a deep breath while in the on-deck circle and repeat it before they step into their *positive rectangle*. By doing so, the hitter will clear out negative thoughts and give himself a better opportunity for success.

Pitchers must pitch tension free! A bad call, an error behind him, can create anxiety and tension before the next pitch. He should step back off of the rubber, take a deep breath before he reenters his *positive rectangle*, and take charge of the immediate situation. To help the hitter or pitcher, coaches should not use the term *relax* but replace it with *breathe*. To relax lessens muscle control and does not do much for the mental tension and anxiety of the moment. And taking a deep breath allows the individual to pause a moment to escape from the immediate turmoil and clear out the negative vibes that may have entered the mind. Along with the term *slump*, the term *relax* should be outlawed in your team's lexicon.

> "If you have positive thoughts, positive things will happen."

I didn't say relax out there, I said Breath

JACK R. HELBER

When You Go to the Plate, Do You Have a Hitting Plan?

Every at bat in the game brings with it a different situation. This makes it very important for the hitter to know what his role should be when he steps into the batter's box. The following is an excerpt from Joe Torre's book, *The Yankee Years*.

The setting: 2004 ALCS game 4, Red Sox trail the Yankees 3 games to 0, and 4–3 in the bottom of the ninth at Fenway Park—facing extinction. Kevin Millar leads off for Boston facing Mariano Rivera (the best reliever of his time).

> "I've always had good at bats against Mo," Millar said. "Decent numbers. But you don't want to make a living hitting against him. He's a power guy, and I like the fast ball, so I was just thinking one thing: get a pitch up and middle in, and hit a home run (over the Green Monster) to tie the game. That was my thought process. Just try to hit a home run. There was no looking away. So I was basically in watch mode. If I could just get something up and leaking in, and I was trying to pull, I thought that was our only chance. That's what I felt.
>
> The watch mode served Millar well, because he was only going to swing if the ball entered

the area in which he was watching. Millar actually made himself patient. The downside of this approach is that he essentially conceded the outer half of the plate to Rivera, at least until he got two strikes. Rivera never got two strikes. He missed with his first pitch. Millar fouled off the next. Then Rivera missed with three consecutive pitches, putting the tying runner on base with a free pass.

"You're looking in," Millar said of his approach, "and the thing is, sometimes when you are aggressive at the plate, in an area like that, your hitter's instinct will be to lay off. Whereas, sometimes when you think you have to cover too much of the plate, you start chasing more. I was actually looking for one pitch; I was looking 'dead red' and in…"

Ending scene: Dave Roberts's pinch ran and stole second and scored on a base hit by Bill Mueller to tie the game. The Red Sox won in the twelfth. They won the next three ALCS games versus the Yankees to go to the World Series against the St. Louis Cardinals. They swept the Cards in four games for an eight-game winning streak to end the 2004 season as world champs.

The point here is not to necessarily go to the plate looking to hit a home run all the time. The point is to *know the situation of the game when you come to bat every time. Recognize what your role should be, knowing that the role can change on every at bat or pitch. Create a hitting plan, and stay with it until the best possible outcome.*

Andrelton Simmons of the LA Angels has a similar story to tell, after making an adjustment following a poor first half of the season. "Instead of just swinging at strikes, I'm looking for a particular pitch and waiting for that pitch. It doesn't happen all the time, but I've been doing a better job because I'm swinging at better pitches. I'm trying to shrink the zone of what I'm looking for, and it's helping."

Shrink the zone! Players get an average of twelve to fourteen pitches in a 7-inning game (sixteen pitches in a 9-inning game). Make the most of those pitches and increase your walk rate while lowering your strikeout percentages. When you go to the plate, know what you are looking for and wait to get it. Take a strike if it's not what you want. Have patience. If you have two strikes on you, learn to get a piece of the ball and foul it off, then look for the next pitch to be yours. As mentioned earlier, it won't happen every at bat, but the odds are in your favor.

> "Life will always throw you curves, just keep fouling them off. The right pitch will come along, and when it does, be prepared to run the bases."

BASEBALL PSYCHOLOGY: THE GRAY MATTER FACTOR

Fine Centering the Senses

Fine centering is a way of using the senses for complete efficiency. It can be used with any of the five senses—touch, smell, hearing, taste, and vision. In baseball, we use the technique of *fine centering* with the sense of vision, especially at the plate, as a hitter. When in the batter's box, the hitter must (1) concentrate—block out all movements and noises that could be distracting, (2) visualize a spot on the pitcher—usually the letter on his cap or the top of the shoulder of his throwing arm, and fine-center (concentrate) solely on that spot until (3) as the pitcher's hand comes up to deliver the pitch, transfer that concentration to the ball in his hand. This concentration should enable you to see the ball clearer and follow it better and to pick up movements of certain pitches earlier and easier. Increasing visual skills should help in increasing your batting average. Pitchers can also benefit by using this fine-center technique by concentrating on the catcher's target as he pitches. You can practice fine centering skills using other senses such as sound. When you are in a room or in a park, pick out a specific sound other than the dominating sounds and center on it. The lesser sound will become more intense.

> "Self-confidence takes discipline and focus."

Tracking and Pitch Recognition

Tracking is an exercise in which the hitter follows the pitch from the pitcher's hand and the release of the ball into the catcher's glove, especially if you do not swing at the pitch. By doing this, the hitter will be able to see the movement on a certain pitch and see what the umpire may be calling. This information can be used later in the game. Each pitcher has his own repertoire of pitches—those pitches he usually relies on. He will use various grips to throw three types of fast balls (4-seamer, 2-seamer, cutter), sliders, curves, change ups, and a few other specialty pitches. By tracking the pitch, the hitter can gain an idea as to what pitches he may see and an early realization of what to expect from the pitcher. This can give the hitter an advantage.

Pitch recognition means exactly what it says. It is the second phase of tracking, which is recognizing the pitch that is being delivered. This can be practiced in a drill. A player throws a pitch to a batter standing maybe twenty feet away. The pitch is either a fast ball (reduced speed) or a curve ball. The batter calls the pitch fast ball or curve ball and then tracks the pitch into the glove of the third player acting as a catcher. Once the ball is in the catcher's glove, the batter will then swing at where the strike pitch went through the zone. If the pitch was not a strike, the batter will not swing. It is to a young hitter's advantage to work on these techniques as they can only become better at a very difficult thing to do—using a round bat to hit a round ball traveling at a very high speed with various movements.

> "Big things are accomplished through
> the perfection of minor details!"
> —John Wooden

Your Memory Bank

When a young boy or girl gets their first job and makes some money, they might put away a few dollars into a piggy bank of sorts for safe keeping. As time goes by, and they get older, they will open a savings account at a local bank. In baseball, the same scenario should apply. As a player progresses through their playing career and learns new nuances of the game, they should create a *memory bank* and store this new knowledge for use the next time similar situations arise. This bank should remain open for the rest of the playing career. Not just the big ideas but also the smallest of thoughts that for some reason always show up at the strangest times.

As the player moves throughout his career and continues to build up his *memory bank* account, he will find that the dividends he will receive will be large and could propel him farther up the chain. It would be a good idea for a player to keep a personal book of notes at home where he can jot down certain baseball information that he may have learned in that day's game. This would become a major resource for him. Drawing out what has been learned and maintained can go a long way toward developing an *instinct* toward resolving situations that occur instantaneously on the field. This is referred to as *baseball savvy*.

> "There is no win or lose. It's win or learn!"

Become a Junkie

Through the years, you've established a *memory bank*. Hopefully it has become chock-full of valuable memories and lessons learned during your time in baseball. Memories of situations and how you dealt with them to overcome difficult moments. Lessons you have learned, while playing, that you can use on the field again and again. These are important and very valuable toward your career development as a player, but another critical lesson that you must work on to become a leader is to learn the rules of the game. Knowing the rules will help guide you through many situations that can occur on the field. It will help you in making decisions on the field based on your experiences. The game is filled with rules and regulations, and a player who is knowledgeable of these tricky rules will have an advantage. Start by taking time to read the rule book. You will be enlightened by many strange things that can happen in the game. Pay attention to certain situations that occur during your games and how they were resolved.

Another interesting idea for a *baseball junkie* is to become a Little League umpire in your local leagues. This will give you an opportunity to apply the rules and will give you an idea of what an umpire has to experience. You will gain more respect for that person especially when he is working a game that you are playing. When your teammates learn that you are a *junkie*, they will respect you more and at times turn to you for guidance. You don't have to preach what you know, just apply that knowledge when the situation arises. This is where the respect will develop. This respect will flow over into the community as they see that you are giving back to the young, up-and-coming players what you were given.

It will become the beginning of another life cycle for you.

> "The difference between who you are and who you want to be, is what you do!"

Doing the Little Things

Every team, every player can or perform the "big" things in baseball. Running, throwing, pitching, catching, and hitting are part of every player's ability, to a certain degree. Baseball scouts, whether they are Little League coaches or major league scouts, are always looking for the "big 5" in ability. However, all of those skills can be easily enhanced if the player will take the time to work hard and refine his abilities. Start in the weight room strengthening legs and arms with a proper regimen that is suited for baseball.

More importantly, observe and listen to coaches, and even more experienced players, when they perform or speak. They have been where you are now. They can give you a true insight into the performance of a skill. They have learned the "tricks of the trade"! The best way to turn a double play, importance of hitting to the opposite field, footwork on fielding a ground ball, how to field a fly ball and make a throw, the best way to block a pitch, and many many more "tricks" can be learned from these experienced players. There are so many more things you can learn to gain an advantage. Listen and learn! And when you hear something new to you, put it into your *memory bank*.

In baseball, there are three main skills that are performed in every game: hitting, pitching, defense. Generally speaking, in a game, if a team excels in two of the three in any combination, it will have a great chance for success. For the season, this same principle is true. If a team does well in two of those categories, a team can expect a positive ending to the season. Each player on a team needs to take what they do best and hone those skills for the betterment of the team. Remind your players to work the hardest on those skills they do best. Those skills can be put together with the skills of teammates to create a highly efficient team.

> "The last Froot Loop in a bowl of milk is always the hardest to catch."

BASEBALL PSYCHOLOGY: THE GRAY MATTER FACTOR

Seven Rules to Winning Ways

As baseball has been played throughout the years, it has been determined that there are seven distinct guidelines that teams should follow in order to be successful. They are called Seven Rules to Winning Ways.

(1) First Pitch Strikes: it is important for the pitcher to get ahead of the count as it will help him determine what pitches he can use to get the hitter out. Working ahead of the count is a boon to the success of the pitcher. A 70 percent first pitch strike (fps) is a goal for which a pitcher and the entire staff should aim.

(2) This rule also rests on the pitcher's shoulder. No Two Out Walks: a base on balls with two outs is a freebie and can lead to a disastrous inning. The door is open for the opposition to get a rally started. It is even worse if there are already runners on bases. Many times a team has parlayed a two out walk into a scoring inning.

(3) Make the Routine Plays: the player who makes a great play on the field is exciting to watch, but the athlete who becomes a steady reliable defensive player is more valuable to his team. Mishandling a routine ground ball with two outs is a "killer" for a team.

(4) Keep the Double Play Alive: the double play is the most important play of the game. It keeps the pitcher out of trouble. Every player of the field has a role in keeping the double play alive. The middle

infielders (shortstop and second base) are key players in turning double plays because one of them will be the pivot man who relays to first base. Outfielders must make decisions, with more than one runner on, whether to throw ahead of the lead runner on a play he feels he can throw out the runner, or throw behind the runner to keep the double play alive not allowing the trail runner to advance. Keeping the double play alive is critical toward winning a game.

(5) After a Big Inning, Get a "Shutdown" Inning: when a team scores several runs in an inning and returns to field on defense, it is their goal to not give any runs back. Score 3, 4, 5 runs in an inning, hit the field, and shut the opponent out the following half inning.

(6) Win the One-Run Games: Many times the win–loss success of a season can be traced to the team's ability to win the one-run games, 3–2, 4–3, etc. When it comes down to the end of the season, these one-run games will become critical to a team's chances to advance.

(7) You Gotta Beat the Bottom Clubs: simply put, you cannot allow the last place teams to beat you. A combination of one-run losses and losing to the last place team will sound a death knell for a team.

"Number one rule, attend to business."
—Lefty Grove

One Step Beyond

From the beginning, your mother and father preached *hard work*. Hard work was the key to success in life. As you progressed through your schooling, they tried to push you to do your best. If you became involved in a sports team—any sport—or joined the band, cheerleading team, or some club, your parents pushed you to work hard on that activity. Your coach would also preach hard work, saying that it is what you had to do to become proficient to reach the top in your sport or activity. They know this because each sport is competitive, and if you don't work hard, the other guy will win the job. By pushing you, it will make you a better player. The coach also knows a better "you" will make the team a better "we," which can lead to a better season. This push for hard work reflects later in life when you manage to secure a job. You will find that a job becomes just as competitive as a sport, and you have to work hard to advance on the job. Hard work is critical, but there is more.

On your team, you must find an edge, something that makes you standout. To do this, you must search within yourself to determine what makes up your personality, and what it is that will give you an edge in relating with your teammates. When you are able to determine these things, you will have a better opportunity to establish influence on your teammates, and more importantly become a better athlete. Become an advocate for your team, show them that you are all in for a positive outcome for you and your teammates. Let them know, and let them see that you want to become the best athlete that you can, for the benefit of the team. Encourage them through difficult moments and show them that you can survive challenging times also. Help your team develop a *swag*. A team togetherness that says, we can play this game too!

When you can create your own edge, and develop positive perceptions of you, you will have taken the *one step beyond* towards becoming a great athlete and leader. Set a trend whereby your teammates will follow you through all situations. Control your responses such as fears, failures, and even excitements, by showing even handedness toward all situations. Show courage through difficult times. Yes, you can show emotion, but express your responses with a positive attitude. Inspire your teammates! Coaches are always looking for these athletes because they know it will make running the team smoother. They know that it will make the team a more cohesive unit and that they will play better and fight for each other toward winning a game. But someone has to be the field leader. Someone has to take charge on the field. It might as well be you. Coaches also know that this type of athlete will become a success at anything they want to do in the future.

> "You don't inspire your teammates by showing them how great you are. You inspire them by showing them how great they are!"

BASEBALL PSYCHOLOGY: THE GRAY MATTER FACTOR

Seventeen Inches

(This is an expression of an idea by Coach John Scolinos of California Polytechnic College in Pomona California at an American Baseball Coaches Convention a few years back. I attended Cal Poly Pomona and he was my coach and mentor.)

There is one constant in America, and in the world for that matter. This constant- a law or rule- does not consider your age, size, gender, or ethnicity. It is a constant that everyone must abide by- there are no exceptions! That constant is the *home plate* in baseball. Home plate in Little League is 17 inches across. In 14U team games, it is seventeen inches; high school, seventeen inches; college, 17 inches; professional baseball and the major leagues- you guessed it- seventeen inches. It is a worldwide standard. However, it is more than that. It is the standard that one should adopt to hold themselves accountable to that which is right and fair to all. It is the standard that tells us we do not change the rules for individuals and that consequences for actions are the same for all individuals. If a pitcher cannot throw the ball over the 17-inch plate, it will not be widened for him. He will simply not pitch. On a team, the coach must adhere to this constant with his players. The top players and team leaders should all be held to the same standards and team rules. If any player cannot follow the rules set forth by the team, the 17-inch plate will not be expanded for him. Every player is equal on the team, and each player will be held accountable for his actions, or sometimes lack of actions.

"Discipline is doing things correctly every single time."

—Tony Muser

Climbing the Ladder

What you learn, and how much you grow, in the game of baseball, and the game of life, is totally up to you. You are in charge. The most a coach can do is show you how and be an advocate for you. The amount of dedication and commitment you give to the learning process will determine your growth. After all is said and done, it is all about how you grow in the game. Work endlessly to *master* the game. It will take hard work, training, competition, and performance. The destination is the ultimate goal. But the fun is what happens on the road to what you want to achieve. The fun comes from conquering frustrations and perservering in situations where you may have had some doubt, but overcame that fear. Once you have reached a feeling that you have *mastered* the game, don't stop. Continue to challenge yourself and go for the next step on the ladder. Remember, your work is never done, it has only begun. There is always something new to learn. The game changes all the time, just as life changes.

To aid in climbing the ladder, set individual goals for yourself. Make them attainable only if you have to work hard to get there. The goals you set should include personal goals including self-awareness, and who you are. And what you represent within your teammates. You can also set statistical goals such as a batting average, runs batted in etc. After you reach the goal, set a new goal with the same desire to *climb the ladder.* Don't be discouraged, but motivate yourself to get better and better. Make each day in practice a chance to become better than yesterday! Set clear goals, discipline yourself to strive for them, and focus on the process it will take to reach them.

> "The journey of a thousand miles begins with a single step"

Believe in Yourself

Life's Creed: Own your own happiness! You are responsible, in your heart, for your happiness. Believe in yourself, believe in your dreams. Preach your dreams, if only to yourself! But share them with others, emotionally and visually. Have confidence that you are going to make them all come true. Make the most of what you are given. Expect to do well! Expect to be a winner. Don't let anyone put you down, and don't allow others to set limits for you! Whatever you do, become the best at what you do. If you don't see yourself with value, nobody else will. Enjoy yourself, and enjoy the journey that life and baseball brings. It's a work ethic and takes a drive to complete, but this is the way to happiness. If you work hard to overcome perceived unfairness in life, remember, "what is taken away once will be given back twice!" In the end only you will be the author of your life's story. The most important factor in helping the young athlete to perform at a high level of efficiency is to create a positive atmosphere around him. Combating the negativism and creating this positive atmosphere is a constant project for the individual, his teammates, and the coaching staff.

> "I'm all smiles watching my players whiz by during their laps on the first day...the promise of a new season ahead. I hope we never lose sight of the fact that this is a game young men play for enjoyment and life long memories of accomplishment."
>
> —Bo Schembechler,
> University of Michigan

> "It's unbelievable how much you don't know about the game you've been playing all your life."
>
> —Mickey Mantle,
> New York Yankees

Extra Innings

You cannot play baseball forever, although there are programs and leagues for the elderly. However, it is the lessons learned on the field that will carry you throughout your life. Learning to fend off frustrations, setbacks, surprise happenings, unexpected occurances, fear of a new development are all part of life. In reverse, there are also many positive and exciting things that will happen throughout your life. These lesson are geared toward you and your personal development throughout. Overcoming frustrations, having doubt but continuing on, and learning how to battle through tough times are key lessons learned from playing the game of baseball. Facing fear head-on without cowering in it's wake must be one of the most important lessons learned.

Baseball will teach you the importance of working hard for excellence. What it takes to advance to a higher level is essential toward moving up in the work force. Self-discipline, focus, and hard work with the ability to be resilient in handling the daily grind are all learned during your baseball experience. The big lesson learned from baseball and the psychological approach is that, you can only control that for which you are responsible. Through baseball you will learn the importance of your response to adverse moments and how to move ahead. On the field, you will develop a feeling of pride after you have succcesfully oveercome an adversity. The same feelings will follow your successes in real life. Your baseball career will teach you perspective, pride, and discipline when handling life's complexities.

> "The battles that count aren't the ones for gold medals. The struggles within yourself-the invisible battles inside all of us- that's where it's at!"
> —Jesse Owens

THOUGHTS TO GET YOU THROUGH TOUGH TIMES

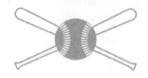

Adversity: not to it, but through it.

To rise above adversity does not build character. It reveals it!

Don't count the innings. Make the innings count!

So what! Next pitch!

You can make excuses, or you can make it happen. But you can't do both.

Losing is an attitude, being behind a temporary situation.

The more you sweat in training, the less you'll bleed in battle- Navy Seals.

"Attitude—too busy to be sad, too positive to be worried, to determined to be defeated!"—P. J. Fleck

Being average doesn't take much work.

"Sing your song, dream your dreams, hope your hopes, and pray your prayers."—Bo Schembechler

If you are the smartest person in the room, you're in the wrong room!

"Timing has a lot to do with the outcome of a rain dance!"

"I don't think much of a man who is not wiser today than he was yesterday."—Abraham Lincoln

"The difference between who you are and who you want to be, is what you do!"

"Instead acting in a negative way to failure, make a commitment to being positive. Build on the little things, a small thing here, a small thing there. Manage the things you have control of, such as performance, and embrace the challenge of baseball."—Ken Ravizza

"Baseball gives every American boy a chance to excel, not just to be as good as someone else, but to be better than someone else. This is the

nature of man and the name of the game."
—Ted Williams, Red Sox

"Babe Ruth was just this magnificent human being. And a really good story because he was this kid who grew up essentially as an orphan, had a tough life, and then went on to become the most successful player ever!"—Bill Bryson, author

"Walk on with hope in your heart, and you'll never walk alone."—song by Elvis Presley

"Every morning, in Africa, a gazelle wakes up. It knows that it better run faster than the fastest lion or it will be killed. Every morning a lion wakes up. It knows that it must run faster than the slowest gazelle or it will starve. It doesn't matter if you are a lion or gazelle, when you wake up, *You better be running*!"—Christopher McDougall, author.

"Happy baseballing."—Coach Boom

REFERENCES

Cain, Brian. *Toilets, Bricks, Fish Hooks and Pride: The Peak Performance Toolbox Exposed.* Scotts Valley, California: CreateSpace, 2013.

Chase, William, and Herbert Simon. "Perception in Chess." *Cognitive Psychology* 4, issue 1 (January 1973): 55–81, https://doi.org/10.1016/0010-0285(73)90004-2.

Crowley, Richard. "How to Cure the Yips." Sportsmaker (website). Last updated September 3, 2015. www.sportsmaker.com.

Dorfman, Harvey. *The Mental Game of Baseball: A Guide to Peak Performance.* South bend, Indiana: Diamond Communications, 2002.

Goldratt, Eliyahu. *Essays on the Theory of Constraints.* Great Barrington, Massachusetts: North River Press, 1998.

Hanson, Tom. *Play Big: Mental Toughness Secrets That Take Baseball Players to the Next Level.* Hanson House, 2020.

Leach, Mike. *Swing Your Sword: Leading the Charge in Football and Life*. New York: Diversion Books, 2011.

Lewis, Michael. *Moneyball: The Art of Winning an Unfair Game*. New York: W. W. Norton & Company, 2003.

Maltz, Maxwell. *Psycho-Cybernetics*. New York: TarcherPerigee, 2015.

McDougall, Christopher. *Born to Run: A Hidden Tribe, Superathletes, and the Greatest Race the World Has Never Seen*. New York: Vintage Books, 2011.

Meier, Jim. *Championship Thinking: Building Mental Muscle in Baseball*. Omaha, Nebraska: Training Connection, 2006.

Orlick, Terry. *In Pursuit of Excellence*. Champaign, Illinois: Human Kinetics Inc., 2015.

Ravizza, Ken, and Tom Hudson. *Heads-Up Baseball: Playing the Game One Pitch at a Time*. New York: McGraw-Hill Education, 1995.

Riffey, Mark. "The Ups and Downs of Complexity." Flathead Beacon (website). Published July 20, 2016. https://flatheadbeacon.com/2016/07/20/ups-downs-complexity.

Rigsby, Rick. "The Wisdom of a Third Grade Dropout" (speech). Uploaded October 5, 2017. https://youtu.be/Bg_Q7KYWG1g.

Ruiz, Miguel. *The Four Agreements: A Practical Guide to Personal Freedom*. San Rafael, California: Amber-Allen Publishing, 2018.

Schembechler, Bo, and John Bacon. *Bo's Lasting Lessons: The Legendary Coach Teaches the Timeless Fundamentals of Leadership*. New York: Grand Central Publishing, 2008.

Torrem, Joe, and Tom Verducci. *The Yankee Years*. New York: Doubleday Books, 2009.

Whiting, Robert. *You Gotta Have Wa*. New York: Vintage Books, 2009.

Wooden, John. *They Call Me Coach*. New York: McGraw-Hill Education, 2003.

Augie Garrido, Texas Longhorns coach

Bob Bennett, head baseball coach (retired), Fresno State, coachbb26@gmail.com

John Scolinos, head coach, Pepperdine University, California Polytechnic State University

BASEBALL AND THE INTANGIBLES

To be athletic takes motor skills and muscle control, but what sets athleticism apart from being a true athlete in a sport is the master of power and control over "the intangibles" of that sport, or any sport. Motor skills and muscle control are the physical aspect of being an athlete while master and control of the intangibles is the mental aspect of being an athlete. Physical prowess cannot function without mental prowess, when becoming an athlete. The following is a list of some intangibles that must be controlled by the athlete. You will find that many are entwined with others.

ATTITUDE: "Who cares?" If you care, you will work hard to improve, to work with your teammates to make yourself and your team the best it can become. If you don't care, you won't be there anyway!

ANXIETY: Occurs when you try too hard, or are too careful not to make an error. Unwind! The best athletes are not perfect, they will make a mistake, but they will shake it off in a very quick time, because the game goes on, and they know they must be ready the next time.

BELIEF: You can only do what you believe you can do, but get the facts- don't thrive on false beliefs, which can be created when you don't TRY! You will be surprised.

CHARACTER: Those features that define great people from little people, the difference lying chiefly "in sacrifice, in self-denial, in love and loyalty, in fearlessness and humility, in the pursuit of excellence and the perfectly disciplined will"- Vince Lombardi. Character is the culmination of the attributes that make up who a person really is. They can't be touched, but they can be seen by observing the individual and his actions.

CONCENTRATION: The discipline that allows one to focus attention on what is happening NOW! and not be concerned with what has happened or will happen. For concentration to be effective, there must be an interest.

CONFIDENCE: An earned feeling that tells you that you can accomplish a task that is in front of you. This feeling of Confidence is gained by the fact that you have been successful in the past so you've done it before.

COURAGE: "Having a goal and understanding the situation are not enough. You must have the courage to act, for only by actions can goals, desires and beliefs be translated into realities."-Admiral William F. Halsey's personal motto.

DESIRE: The will to do what is necessary to be successful in the task at hand. But there is more, "...the greatest accomplishment is not in never failing, but in rising again after you have failed."-Vince Lombardi. Desire is the want to try again and again until success is achieved. Failure is undesired!

EFFORT: Failure is the only thing that can be achieved without effort. Achievement is the sum of attitude, courage, desire and hard work.

EGO: Self-esteem; how you feel about yourself. Ego is good, when it has matured because then, it will lead to emotional stability and a confident approach to any tough situation, and the ability to employ many of the intangibles. A strong healthy ego is the insecticide for fear, frustration.

EMOTION: There is only one basic emotion- excitement-which may appear in the form of fear, anger, courage, etc., depending upon one's inner goals at the time. The real problem is not to control emotion, but to control the choice of which tendency shall receive emotional reinforcement.

FEAR: The insecure emotion that appears when respect should be applied. Fear creates tentative action or reaction, and serves to clutter up the thought processes. You must replace fear with respect.

FRUSTRATION: A symptom of the failure-type personality, which develops whenever some important goal cannot be realized. Continued frustration may mean that the goals we have set for ourselves are unrealistic. Re-evaluate.

GOALS: The point of achievement that establishes success, if you reach it, or failure, if you don't. Therefore, it is important that the goals that one sets for oneself be realistic and within the framework that nature has established.

GRIT: The ability to stay with a difficult situation and fight your way to the succesfull completion.

HABITS: Relaxation of effort, which can be both good and bad. Habits are actions which were formed without the exercise of will power, or effortlessly. Bad habits are the result of the lack of concentration. Good habits take concentration and desire to hone or fine-tune a fundamental action.

INDECISIVENESS: Created by fear of being wrong, and is used for the protection of one's self-esteem. "Big men and big personalities make mistakes and admit them. It is the little man who is afraid to admit he has been wrong."

LUCK: "Luck is the residue of planning and hard work." It is real, created by working hard and being ready for any situation.

OVER-RESPONSE: A reaction created by feelings of fear and anxiety. One must learn to react to pressure situations with respect for it, rather than fear of it.

PERSONALITY: The absolute key to how one absorbs and responds to any given situation. The keys to a success-type personality are the development of clear-cut reasonable goals, the ability to recognize the direction in which improvement lies, and sense to follow that course. Qualities of this type of individual include sense of direction, understanding, courage, clarity, self-esteem and confidence, self-acceptance. Symptoms of the failure-type personality include frustration, loneliness, uncertainty, resentment, insecurity, misdirected aggressiveness, emptiness.

PRESSURE SITUATIONS: The biggest, most dangerous threat to success during periods of crisis is the emotional response- fear. To combat this response, the individual, who thrives on pressure, has learned to recognize the situation for what it is, to develop respect for it, which then allows him to face the crisis and overcome it and defeat it.

PRIDE: A feeling of accomplishment, and the knowing you did well. Outward expression of pride is accepted as long as it does not cross the line into boasting. Having pride in something accomplished can lead to working harder on that act in order to do even better. Pride makes you strive toward perfection- a lofty goal.

RELAXATION: A lack of response. Relaxation of muscles brings about a mental relaxation, which becomes nature's tranquilizer, erecting a barrier between you and the pressure situation. The opposite of tension. The athlete must find a happy medium between relaxation and tension in order to function at maximum capability.

RESILIENCE: Grit. The ability to forge your way through tough situations and finally reach success.

RESPECT: The positive replacement for fear. Respect for a pressure situation, rather than fear of it, serves to overcome the negative emotion and anxiety that can develop, and will assist the athlete in the success over that situation.

SELF-CONFIDENCE: The ability to attack a certain task with no fear. The feeling that you can accomplish whatever lies in front of you.

SELF-EXPRESSION: How you openly react to situations, based on your learned experiences and maturity. One's reaction to situations is based entirely on his development and mastering of most of the intangibles listed here. Body language will indicate one's master and maturity of emotional stability.

SELF-IMAGE: Appreciation of your own worth, built upon your own beliefs about yourself. These beliefs have been created through experience and success of the goals that one has set for oneself. This is why, setting of attainable goals is so important in creating a positive feeling toward oneself. Positive success will lead to positive self-esteem.

SELF-PITY: An emotional response of feeling sorry for yourself because you were not immediately successful in an endeavor, putting oneself ahead of the team in importance.

SUCCESS: Having accomplished what you set out to do, whether it is a big task or a small one. This accomplishment will make you feel good, and this feeling, added to more successes, will lead to a positive self-image. Therefore, it is very important, again, to set realistic goals. After a successful experience, you should make sure to record that in your mind-put it in your "memory bank." Success is not determined by wins and losses, but rather by preparing and knowing you have done your best.

TENSION: The body's preparation to act or respond to a situation. The opposite of relaxation, which can be lead to no response at all. In the moment of a pressure situation, tension must be reduced as much as possible- "take a deep breath." To successfully handle the pressure, one must find the proper balance between tension and relaxation.

WILL: Desire. The absolute power that makes you want to succeed. The driving force that pushes the athlete to do whatever is necessary to accomplish a goal.

WINNING FEELING: An aura, developed by keeping a positive goal in mind and thinking of it in terms of an accomplished fact. Self-confidence, courage, faith that the outcome will be desirable. An inner attitude of positive feelings.

As much as these ideas and thoughts are related to baseball and the athletes performance on the field, so too can they relate to life in general. Much of the ideas expressed in this text received stimulus from the book Psycho-Cybernetics, by Dr. Maxwell Maltz.

-----HAPPY BASEBALLING---- COACH HELBER

METAPHYSICS
OF SUCCESS

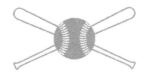

1. ON PREPARATION: Want to learn. Be prepared to improve. Never be satisfied. Do not accept mediocrity. Take care of your body; eat well and get rest. Make sacrifices necessary to make you a better player and the team a better team.

2. ON ONENESS: Be a teammate. Never let a teammate down. Acknowledge your teammates successes, even if he is playing your position. Your teammates succes can only make your job easier. Care! Do not accept less than all you can give from yourself. Do not accept less from your teammates. Push each other.

3. ON MENTAL TOUGHNESS: Poise, patience, endurance. Every problem has a solution. Be part of that solution. Never give in. Equipment throwing, profanity, and temper tantrums do not display poise. Be in charge, don't allow emotions to take over. It is a negative game. Learn to handle failure, fear, and frustration. Analyze, stay focused and poised.

4. ON HUSTLE: "Hustle is a talent." Hustle creates team spirit; it inspires. Be intense and contribute to the "pulse of the game." Expect nothing less from your teammates. *Physical hustle* includes running out every fly ball, wind sprint, working hard in drills and in the cages, even when no coach is nearby. "Luck is the residue of hard work." Get Lucky! *Mental hustle* includes interest, enthusiasm, aggressiveness, single mindedness toward reaching a goal.

5. ON CONCENTRATION: Stay focused on the job at hand. Know the game's situation at all times. It is a daily three hour job, practice or game. Put your full effort into it- no moms, no dads, no friends, just you, your teammates, and your coaches.

6. ON RESPONSIBILITY: Be loyal to your teammates and coaches for they are the ones to whom you are responsible. Trust each other. No one is going to make a mistake intentionally. Follow the rules. Be on time. Hustle in practice. Do not second guess your teammates or coaches. Do not make negative comment s towards your teammates. Do not "trash talk" your opponent. Represent your team on and off the field. Be a positive role model on your campus and in your community. Be DRUG FREE! Look well groomed. Attend all team functions.

7. ON EFFORT: Effort should never cease. Spend energy on those things over which you have control. Don't waist time on situations over which you have no control. Work hardest on the things that you do

BEST! Excel in something! "Only mediocre people feel they are aloways doing their best." Do not accept mediocrity- except it! Nothing is effortless.

THE FOUR AGREEMENTS

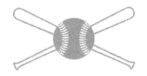

DR. DION MIGUEL RUIZ

1. **BE IMPECCABLE WITH YOUR WORD:**
   Speak with Integrity. Say only what you mean. Avoid using the word to speak against yourself or gossip about others. Use the answer of your word in the direction of truth and love.
   BASEBALL INTERPRETATION: *Love your teammates. Do not speak negatively of them, you need them for the success of the team. Be honest and forthright with your teammates when interacting with them.*

2. **DON'T TAKE ANYTHING PERSONALLY:**
   Nothing others do is because of you. What others say and do is a projection of their dreams. When you are immune to the opinions and actions of others, you won't be the victim of needles suffering.

BASEBALL INTERPRETATION: *Each player is responsible for their actions and opinions. This should not affect your performance, on field decisions, or opinions. When you grasp this concept it will make you free of outside interferences and negative feelings.*

3. **DON'T MAKE ASSUMPTIONS:** Find the courage to ask questions and express what you really want. Communicate with others as clearly as you can to avoid misunderstandings, sadness and drama. With just this one agreement, you can completely transform your life.
BASEBALL INTERPRETATION: *Communication is the key to understanding. If you don't know or understand why or how something is done on the field, ask questions so there can be no misunderstandings. Others may have the same questions. Knowing the answers can only make it easier for you to perform the task on the field.*

4. **ALWAYS DO YOUR BEST:** Your best is going to change from moment to moment; it will be different when you are healthy as opposed to sick. Under any circumstances, simply do your best, and you will avoid self-judgement, self-abuse, and regret.
BASEBALL INTERPRETATION: *If your teammates know you are trying to do your best under all circumstances, you will only gain their respect as well as your own self-respect.*

Dr. Miguel Ruiz is a Mexican shamanist of Toltec spiritualism. Born in 1952 and has a book released in March of 2017.

WHAT OTHER PEOPLE HAVE SAID

'Whoever wants to know the heart and mind of America had better learn baseball!- Jacques Barzun, Columbia Univ.

"Baseball, it is said, is only a game. True. And the Grand Canyon is only a hole in Arizona."- George F. Will

Be quick, don't hurry"- John Wooden UCLA Basketball coach.

"He's dangerous when he is using the whole field!" - Miguel Cabrera, Detroit Tigers.

"God helped you get to the plate. The rest is up to you."- Ted Williams, Boston Red Sox

"Hustle is a talent."- Bill Russell, Boston Celtics

"There has always been hard times. There have always been wars and troubles- famine, disease, and such- and some folks are born with money and some with none. In the end, it is up to the Man (Woman) what they become, and none of those other things matter!"- Billy Graham, Evangelist.

"It's not all about talent. It's about dependability, consistancy, and understanding what you need to do to improve."- Bill Belichick, New England Patriots

"I loved the game. I loved the competition. But I never had fun. I never enjoyed it. All hard work, all the time."- Carl Yastrzemski, Boston Red Sox.

"Timing has a lot to do with the outcome of a rain dance."-Texas Bix Bender

"You may get 10 swings in a game but it only takes one swing to make a difference!"- Babe Ruth

"When I was a small boy in Kansas, a friend of mine and I went fishing. I told him I wanted to be a real major league baseball player, a genuine professional like Honas Wagner. My friend said that he'd like to be President of the United States. Neither one of us got our wish!"- Dwight D. Eisenhower, 34th President of the United States.

"There have only been two geniuses in the world. Willie Mays and Willie Shakespeare."-Tallulah Bankhead, actress.

"Think! How in the heck are you gonna hit and think at the same time?"- Yogi Berra, New York Yankees

"One thing that will help you become a better hitter is the pitches you don't swing at!"

"Naturally, I think baseball is the most admirable pastime in the world. A keen combination of wit, intelligence, and muscle. It develops the mind, establishes discipline and gives to those who take part in it, sound bodies, clear heads, and a better sense of life."- John J. McGraw, 1908.

"There are 108 beads in a Catholic Rosary, and there are 108 stitches in a basebsll. When I heard that, I gave Jesus a chance."- from 'Bull Durham.'

"America has rolled by like an army of steamrollers. It's been erased like a blackboard, rebuilt and erased again. But baseball has marked the time. This field, this game is part of our past. It reminds us of everything that was once good, and could be good again. If you build it, people will come, Ray, oh most definitely, they will come."- from 'Field of Dreams.'

"Practice does not make perfect! Only perfect practice makes perfect."- Vince Lombardi, Green Bay Packers

"Ability is what you are capable of doing. Motivation determines what you do with it. Attitude determines how well you do it.!"- Lou Holtz, Notre Dame

"Whether you are a Siamese cat or a black alley cat makes no difference, as long as you can catch mice!" - Ding Chou Ping, Chinese Emperor

"Surround yourself with good people. Don't mess with donkies!"- John Scolinos, Cal Poly Pomona

"To each there comes, in their lifetime, a special moment when they are figuratively tapped on the shoulder and offered the chance to do a very special thing, unique to them and fitted to there talents. What a tragedy if that moment finds them unprepared or un-qualified for that which could have been their finest hour!"- Sir Winston Churchill

EPILOGUE

Making Fun of It: The definition of *fun* in baseball (or any sport) is the ability to walk off of the field with a feeling that you played a good game and did the best that you could. You played the game *right*, or as it should be played. It has been mentioned in this text that the player should have *fun* playing the game, simply by participation. "W's" and "L's" are a goal but, in reality, they cannot be achieved without having *fun*. Playing a sport in school is a voluntary act, therefore, coaches should create practices which accomplish fundamental excellence as well as creating team spirit. An avid young player, who is learning the nuances of the game, wants to do everything he can to help improve his abilities, and is willing to work hard on each aspect of the game. There are many ways to approach fundamental baseball skills that the coach can use and that will make it *FUN* for the young player, in a tension free atmosphere.

PING PONG: Ping Pong is a great game for hand-eye coordination, especially early in the season.

Players can compete in doubles or singles in a tournament organized by the coach, creating competition and spirited inner-team rivalry.

ULTIMATE FRISBEE: Another game of inner-team competition using only the flip of the frisbee to make a throw. This will teach hitters to get their hands through when swinging a bat, as it is the same motion.

SKIPPING ROCKS: Infielders can go down to the river or lake and compete in a rock skipping contest, using throwing techniques that they will need in making throws in the infield.

CHESS: Early in the season, or when the field is not available, is a good time for players to *practice* "making decisions.," an activity which is not emphasized much in the game, but is the first thing a player must do when a ball is hit to him in the field- how am I going to make this play? Someone on the team knows how to play chess, so have them teach the team. Set time limits to make a move (15-30 seconds)- the shorter the better. It will be a challenge and a chess tournament will create more team morale.

ONE EYED JACKS: Another competitive game to play, following batting practice. Group is divided into two teams. One on the field, one at bat. A batting practice pitcher will pitch. Only one base is used in this game- 2B. Batters hit and run straight to second and back. They can be forced out, thrown out, or fly ball outs. 6 outs to an inning. Here they get extra batting practice, and compete with little tension. It's fun, and the players will be able to loosen up from a more strict practice session.

These are only a few ideas that the coach can use to help young players understand the game. They provide for inner-team spirited competition, and a tension free segment of the practice. Coaches can come up with other ideas that will work to help their players approach the game with a positive attitude.

CPSIA information can be obtained
at www.ICGtesting.com
Printed in the USA
BVHW032325010322
630318BV00008B/658

9 781648 951725